The World's Most AMAZING BUILDINGS

PAUL MASON

www.raintreepublishers.co.uk
Visit our website to find out more information about **Raintree** books.

To order:
☎ Phone 44 (0) 1865 888112
📄 Send a fax to 44 (0) 1865 314091
💻 Visit the Raintree bookshop at **www.raintreepublishers.co.uk** to browse our catalogue and order online.

First published in Great Britain by
Raintree, Halley Court, Jordan Hill,
Oxford OX2 8EJ, part of Harcourt
Education. Raintree is a registered
trademark of Harcourt Education Ltd.

© Harcourt Education Ltd 2007
First published in paperback in 2007.
The moral right of the proprietor has been asserted.

Editorial: Louise Galpine, Rosie Gordon,
Dave Harris, and Stig Vatland
Design: Victoria Bevan and Bigtop
Picture Research: Mica Brancic and Elaine Willis
Production: Camilla Crask

Originated by Chroma Graphics Pte. Ltd
Printed and bound in China by WKT

10 digit ISBN 1 406 20355 6 (hardback)
13 digit ISBN 978 1 4062 0355 4
11 10 09 08 07
10 9 8 7 6 5 4 3 2 1

10 digit ISBN 1 406 20376 9 (paperback)
13 digit ISBN 978 1 4062 03769
12 11 10 09 08
10 9 8 7 6 5 4 3 2 1

**British Library Cataloguing in
Publication Data**

Mason, Paul, 1967–
The world's most amazing buildings. – (Atomic)
720
A full catalogue record for this book is available
from the British Library.

Acknowledgements

The publishers would like to thank the following for
permission to reproduce photographs: Alamy. pp. **29**
(Greg Bast), **22** (Pixonnet.com/Bo Jansson); Corbis,
p. **9 main**; Corbis pp. **15**, **17** (Richard Berenholtz), **16**
(Bettmann), **18 main** (L Clarke), **6** (Paul Hardy), **14** (Bob
Krist), **9 inset** (Richard T Nowitz), **23** (Hans Strand), **18
inset** (Paul A. Souders); European Space Agency, p. **25**;
Getty Images, pp. **11 inset** (Hulton Archive), **26 bottom**
(Stone), **5** (Stone/ James Strachan); Lonely Planet Images,
p. **11 main**; Masterfile/ R Ian Lloyd, p. **12**; National
Oceanic & Atmospheric Administration (NOAA), p. **21
top**; Rex Features/Bob Shanley, p. **21 bottom**; www.
treesort.com, p. **26 top**. Cover photograph reproduced
with permission of Corbis (Michael Freeman) **(top)**; Getty
Images (Taxi) **(bottom)**.

The publishers would like to thank Diana Bentley,
Nancy Harris, and Dee Reid for their assistance in the
preparation of this book.

Every effort has been made to contact copyright holders
of any material reproduced in this book. Any omissions
will be rectified in subsequent printings if notice is given
to the publishers.

Disclaimer

Contents

Some words are printed in bold, **like this**. You can find out
what they mean in the glossary. You can also look in the box
at the bottom of the page where the word first appears.

AMAZING ARCHITECTURE

Walk along a street near where you live. If every street was identical, the world would be a very dull place. Fortunately, there are a lot of different, exciting buildings around.

Different buildings

All over the world there are amazing buildings, such as giant skyscrapers, a hotel made of ice, and even a whole town built underground. There are ancient **tombs** that celebrate dead leaders and huge theatres that used to hold real-life fights to the death.

Some people take a holiday in a tree house. Others spend time living in a 'house' at the bottom of the sea. Some people even live in space!

How high?

Look for this box to find out how high each building is.

Work on Sagrada Família cathedral in Barcelona, Spain, started in the 1880s and is still not finished today.

tomb   place like a room where a dead body is buried

Egypt

What does the Great Pyramid weigh?

The Great Pyramid weighs around 6.5 million tonnes.

That's about the same as:

✴ one million tyrannosaurus rex all piled on top of one another, or

✴ 48,000 blue whales.

The Great Pyramid was finished in 2489 BCE. It was built in only 20 years, using simple tools and muscle power.

THE GREAT PYRAMID AT GIZA

The Great Pyramid in Egypt is 4,500 years old. For almost 4,000 of those years it was the tallest building on Earth.

Treasures of the Pyramid

The Pyramids were built to protect the **tombs** of Egyptian rulers. Mountains of gold and jewels were stored in hidden chambers. Secret passageways, dead ends, and disguised doorways were built to discourage thieves. Even so, **tomb robbers** managed to get inside and steal all the treasure.

How high?
The Great Pyramid
140 metres
(459 feet)

tomb robber thief who steals treasure from tombs, especially from the tombs of dead Egyptian rulers

THE COLOSSEUM

The Colosseum in Rome, Italy, was built for public entertainment such as gladiatorial contests. It could accommodate 50,000 spectators.

Entertainment!

Back then (in about 80 CE), people were not interested in football matches. They wanted to see **executions**, men fighting wild animals, and gladiators killing each other.

The Colosseum had many underground tunnels, which were used to house wild animals. These animals would suddenly be let loose to join in the battle.

Amazing fact

The Colosseum had a sandy floor – partly to soak up all the blood!

execution	putting someone to death as punishment for a crime
gladiator	person in Ancient Rome who fought other gladiators, sometimes to the death
spectator	person watching something, such as a sporting event

Italy

The upper seats were for poor people.

The lower seats were for rich and powerful people.

Even though the Colosseum is now a ruin, it is still an amazing building.

How high?

The Colosseum
48 metres
(157 feet)

SALADIN'S CASTLE

Saladin's castle was one of the strongest buildings of its day. Some of its walls are 5 metres (16 feet) thick – thick enough to hide an elephant inside!

The best defence

Attackers had to cross a ditch 28 metres (92 feet) deep. Once the attackers got across the ditch, more hazards were waiting:

* Towers allowed defenders to rain arrows, rocks and boiling oil down on the attackers.

* A gate designed to hold back armies of men stood at the main entrance.

* Narrow passageways meant that the attackers were pushed together, making them easier to kill.

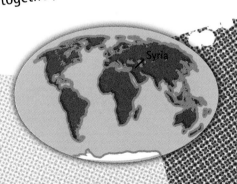

Syria

gorge	deep and narrow valley, with very steep sides
Muslim	person who follows the religion of Islam

Saladin's castle stands on high ground, with a deep gorge on each side.

SALADIN

BORN   1138

DIED   1193

Saladin was a great Muslim warrior and leader.

Australia

Underground homes stay warm at night and cool during the day.

Outside night-time temperatures are below 0 °C (32 °F).

Outside daytime temperatures are over 50 °C (122 °F).

A Town Underground

Coober Pedy is a town in the Australian desert. Its name is said to mean "white man in a hole" in the language of the local Aboriginal people.

From mines to homes

Coober Pedy got its name because **opals** were discovered there in 1916, and since then people have been mining the area. There are now over 250,000 old mines. Consequently, it can be hazardous to walk around in these areas because the ground is weak and full of holes.

To shelter from the extreme desert temperatures, people began to use old mines as houses. Soon, underground homes, shops, and even a church were being specially built.

Over half the people of Coober Pedy live underground.

Amazing fact

Coober Pedy has only had a regular water supply since 1985!

Aboriginal	native people of Australia
opal	type of precious stone

France

There are 1,652 steps to the top of the Eiffel Tower, but most people use the lift!

How High

The Eiffel Tower
300 metres
(984 feet)

Amazing facts

- The Tower was built between 1887 and 1889, by 300 workers.
- 18,038 pieces of iron were used.
- It took 2.5 million rivets to join all the parts of the Tower together.

THE EIFFEL TOWER

The Eiffel Tower in Paris opened in 1889. At 300 metres (984 feet) high, it became the world's tallest building.

For sale!

In 1925, a man called Victor Lustig "sold" the Eiffel Tower for **scrap metal**. He pretended that the government could not afford to keep it anymore. There was one major issue, he did not actually own it! A scrap metal dealer paid Lustig, who quickly escaped on a train, carrying a suitcase full of cash. Lustig got away with it because the man who had "bought" it was too embarrassed to report him!

The **conman** "Count" Victor Lustig (who was not really a Count at all!).

conman	person who tricks other people into giving them money
scrap metal	metal that can be recycled, normally by melting it down and using it to make a new metal object

THE EMPIRE STATE BUILDING

In 1931, the Empire State Building opened in New York. At 381 metres (1,250 feet) high, it became the new world's tallest building.

Getting to the top

Visitors to the Empire State Building can take a lift to the 86th floor to admire the view from 320 metres (1,050 feet). For an even more amazing view, there is another observation platform on the 102nd floor. Most people take one of the 73 lifts to the top, but it is also possible to climb the 1,860 steps.

The Empire State Building has starred in a lot of films, including *King Kong*. In this film, a giant gorilla scales the outside of the building, and fighter planes take off to defend it.

Some of the men who built the Empire State Building take a high-rise lunch break.

There are 6,500 windows in the Empire State Building.

—United States

Amazing facts

■ The Empire State Building cost nearly £14.5 million ($25 million) to build.

■ In 2002, it was sold for £32 million ($57 million)!

How high?

The Empire State Building 381 metres (1,250 feet)

The Sydney Opera House is Australia's most famous building.

Australia

The stages are sheltered by shell-like roofs.

1,056,000 white and cream roof tiles were shipped all the way from Sweden.

THE SYDNEY OPERA HOUSE

No other building looks like the Sydney Opera House. Some people say the roofs resemble giant sails in the harbour. Others say they look like segments of an orange!

Budget breaker

The Opera House almost did not get built. The **architect** who designed it was forced to abandon the project before it was finished. The building took ten years longer than planned and cost over ten times as much as planned. It was supposed to open in 1963 at a cost of £3.5 million ($7 million). It eventually opened in 1973 at a cost of £59 million ($102 million).

Amazing fact

In 1997, climber Alain Robert scaled the Opera House using only sticky climbing shoes.

architect   someone who designs buildings

AQUARIUS

Aquarius is a very unusual kind of building – it is underwater! Aquarius serves as a temporary home to scientists who want to investigate life in the oceans.

Coming and going

Divers enter and leave *Aquarius* in an unusual manner. They use a "wet porch", a room with a hole in the floor. The air pressure inside *Aquarius* stops water from coming in. When someone wants to leave, they just jump through the hole and swim away!

Aquarius is currently deployed near Key Largo, Florida. However, since it can be moved, it will probably be sent to explore other areas of the ocean in the future.

How low?

Aquarius
19 metres
(63 feet)
underwater

United States

Aquarius is held to the seabed by metal plates buried in the sand.

In 2005, Aquarius survived the destruction caused by hurricanes Katrina and Rita.

A large porthole provides a spectacular view of ocean life.

seabed   bottom of the sea

The outside temperature is a very cold -40 °C (-40 °F).

Steel arches support the blocks of ice.

Some ice blocks weigh 2 tonnes.

Reindeer skins over the doors help to keep heat in.

sculpture   work of art usually shaped by carving or moulding material into a new shape

THE ICE HOTEL

The north of Sweden is home to an extraordinary hotel. This amazing structure is constructed almost entirely of ice and snow!

Build and build again

Every winter, the Ice Hotel is completely rebuilt. Ice artists come from around the world to help with the work, carving doors and windows, furniture, and **sculptures**. As a result, every year the Ice Hotel becomes a new and enchanting tourist destination.

The Ice Hotel has a church where weddings are held and a theatre where plays are performed. When the weather warms up in June, the hotel completely melts away.

The inside temperature is only -5 °C (23 °F).

INTERNATIONAL SPACE STATION

The International Space Station (ISS) hovers in **orbit**, hundreds of kilometres above the Earth. The first section was launched into space in 1998, but ISS is still not complete.

An expensive trip

The ISS was designed as a place for scientists to carry out experiments that could not be done on Earth. However, some people argue that the amount of research that is actually done is not worth the huge cost of the space station. Tourists can also visit, but it is only millionaires who can afford it! A trip to the ISS is said to cost over £12 million ($20 million).

orbit	repeated route around something. For example, the Moon is in orbit around the Earth.
solar panel	glass panel that turns the Sun's energy into energy we can use, usually electricity

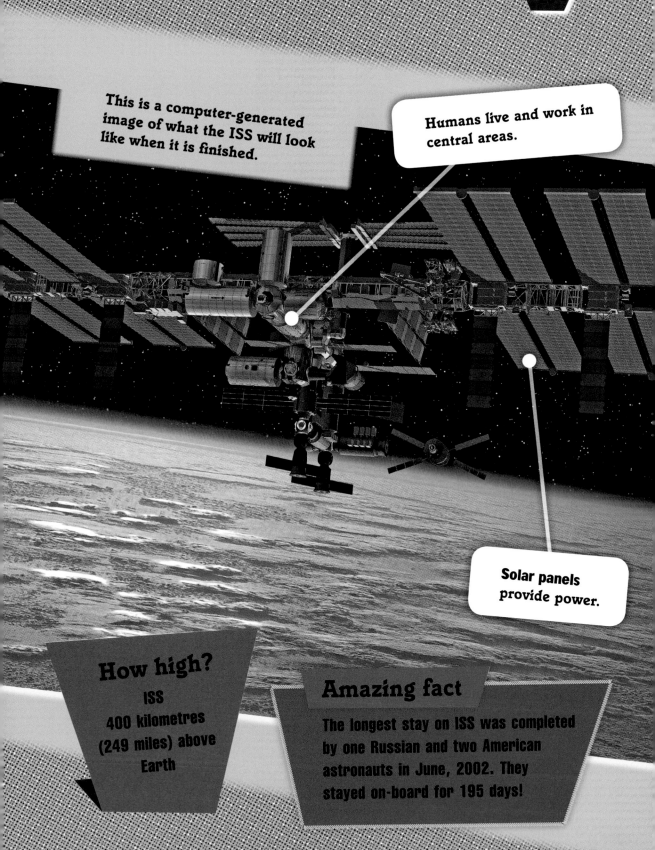

United States

This is one of the tree houses guests can stay in. Grown-ups are allowed, as well as children!

This zip line would be an exciting way to leave the house in the morning.

LIFE IN THE BRANCHES

A lot of children dream of having their own tree house. In Takilma, Oregon, is the "Treesort" – a holiday resort for people who love tree houses!

A house in the sky

The Treesort's different tree houses include a "Treepee" (teepee up a tree), a pirate ship, and a Western saloon. For a school with a difference, you could try the Treehouse Institute of Takilma, a high school that hangs from the branches of an oak tree.

Some walkways between the tree houses are up to 10 metres (32 feet) off the ground and 27 metres (90 feet) long! If you are in a hurry to get back to ground level, you can whiz down a zip line!

How high?
The highest tree house is 11 metres (37 feet) from the ground.

THE WORLD'S TALLEST BUILDING

Taipei 101 is the world's tallest building. If 100 male giraffes could somehow manage to stand on each other's heads, they might just be able to see over the top!

A lucky design

Taipei 101 was based on traditional Chinese design. In China and Taiwan, the number eight is thought to be lucky, so the building has eight tiers and each tier has eight stories. The building also has four circles near the base which are supposed to represent coins. It is hoped that these will bring success to any businesses that operate inside the building.

The diagram below shows how Taipei 101 compares to some of the other buildings in this book.

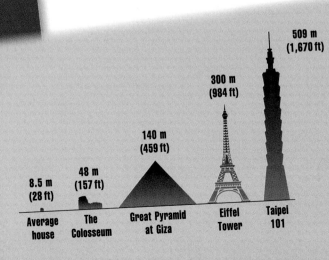

509 m
(1,670 ft)

300 m
(984 ft)

140 m
(459 ft)

48 m
(157 ft)

8.5 m
(28 ft)

Average house | The Colosseum | Great Pyramid at Giza | Eiffel Tower | Taipei 101

How high?
Tapei 101
509 m
(1,670 ft)

The world's tallest buildings
1 Taipei 101, Taiwan   509m   1,670ft
2 Petronas Towers, Malaysia   452m   1,483ft
3 Sears Tower, Chicago   442m   1,450ft

Taiwan

A feng shui expert helped to decide how Taipei 101 should be laid out.

feng shui   set of ideas from China saying that if places are arranged in a way that suits the spiritual forces, good luck will follow; if not, bad luck is likely

Glossary

Aboriginal native people of Australia

architect someone who designs buildings

conman person who tricks other people into giving them money

execution putting someone to death as punishment for a crime

feng shui set of ideas from China saying that if places are arranged in a way that suits the spiritual forces, good luck will follow; if not, bad luck is likely

gladiator person in Ancient Rome who fought other gladiators, sometimes to the death

gorge deep and narrow valley, with very steep sides

Muslim person who follows the religion of Islam

opal kind of precious stone. Opals can be any colour, but are often blue or green.

orbit repeated route around something. For example, the Moon is in orbit around the Earth.

scrap metal metal that can be recycled, normally by melting it down and using it to make a new metal object

sculpture work of art usually shaped by carving or moulding material into a new shape

seabed bottom of the sea

solar panel glass panel that turns the Sun's energy into energy we can use, usually electricity

spectator person watching something, such as a sporting event

tomb place like a room where a dead body is buried

tomb robber thief who steals treasure from tombs, especially from the tombs of dead Egyptian rulers

Want to know more?

Books

✳ *Castle*, Christopher Gravett (Dorling Kindersley, 2002)

✳ *Gladiator*, Richard Ross Watkins (Houghton Mifflin, 2000)

✳ *Pyramid*, James Putnam (Dorling Kindersley, 2002)

✳ *Skyscrapers*, Chris Oxlade (Heinemann Library, 2000)

✳ *The International Space Station*, Franklyn Mansfield Branley (William Morrow, 2000)

Websites

✳ www.cultureandrecreation.gov.au/ articles/sydneyoperahouse/ This site tells the amazing story of the Sydney Opera House.

✳ www.nasa.gov/mission_pages/ station/main/index.html This page tells you all about the International Space Station.

✳ www.uncw.edu/aquarius/ Here you can find out about *Aquarius* and its current activities.

If you liked this Atomic book, why don't you try these...?

Index

Notes for adults
Use the following questions to guide children towards identifying features of report text:
Can you find an example of a general opening classification on page 4?
Can you give an example of a generic participant on page 4?
Can you find examples of the details of a building on page 10?
Can you find examples of non-chronological language on page 18?
Can you give examples of present tense language on page 20?